Life Support

Simon Gray was born in Hampshire and was educated at Westminster School and in Canada and France before reading English at Cambridge. His first play was produced in 1967, since when he has had more than thirty plays and a number of film screenplays produced and published; he has also published five novels and three volumes of diaries. His plays for the stage and television are published by Faber in four volumes under the collective title *The Definitive Simon Gray*.

SIMON GRAY

Life Support

faber and faber
LONDON · BOSTON

First published in 1997
by Faber and Faber Limited
3 Queen Square London WC1N 3AU

Typeset by Faber and Faber Ltd
Printed in England by Mackays of Chatham plc, Chatham, Kent

© Simon Gray, 1997

Simon Gray is hereby identified as author of this
work in accordance with Section 77 of the Copyright,
Designs and Patents Act 1988

All rights whatsoever in this play are strictly reserved and applications for
permission to perform it, etc., must be made in advance, before rehearsals
begin, to Judy Daish Associates, 2 St Charles Place, London W10 6EG. No
performance may be given until a licence has been obtained.

A CIP record for this book
is available from the British Library

ISBN 0–571–19343–9

2 4 6 8 10 9 7 5 3 1

For Nigel

Characters

Jeff Golding (J. G.)
Gwen Golding
Pat O'Brien
Jack Golding
Julia

Life Support was first performed at the Yvonne Arnaud Theatre, Guildford, on 10 June 1997, presented by Duncan Weldon. The cast was as follows:

J. G. Alan Bates
Gwen Georgina Hale
Pat Frank McCusker
Jack Nickolas Grace
Julia Carole Nimmons

Director Harold Pinter
Set designer Eileen Diss
Lighting designer Mick Hughes

SCENE ONE

Lights down.

J. G. (*over*) If everything had worked out all right, I would have been describing a scene something like this. There I am, sitting in the armchair, checking through the contents of my knapsack, my plane tickets, my passport, my vaccination certificate – and suddenly she comes into the room. From the kitchen, of course. 'OK,' she says. 'OK,' says the little woman, elsewhere also referred to as 'wifey'. 'I'm coming with you this time.' 'Why?' I wonder with my usual air of dependence and devotion. 'Why on earth would you want to waste your time coming with me, sweetling mine?' 'To find out what you get up to when you're on your own, hubby mio.' 'But dearest, dearest heart, you won't find out what I get up to on my own if you come with me.' 'In that case, I'll at least stop you from getting up to whatever you get up to while I'm not there with you. By being there. Won't I?' That's how I might have described it if everything had worked out all right.

Lights up.
    A private room in a hospital. Set in darkness, apart from Gwen in bed, on life support.
    J. G., in his early fifties, is walking up and down in front of set, distraught.
    Pat appears.

Pat Mr Golding. I'm Dr O'Brien. Pat O'Brien. (*holding out his hand*) I'm sure Mr Rolls has told you all there is to know about your wife's condition.

J. G. (*shaking Pat's hand*) Well, there doesn't seem very much to know, according to Mr Rolls. Even where she is, so to speak, in her – her consciousness. Even whether she's there or – or not.

Pat But he did explain that she was alive?

J. G. Yes, but that's about as far as he would go. And he used this phrase 'vegetative state' – I couldn't make out whether that was a diagnosis or –

Pat No, no, I think it's merely the usual description for people in your wife's sort of condition. It really means that nobody, not even Mr Rolls, knows what sort of condition that sort of condition is. At least at this stage. I'd like to say how sorry I am, how terribly sorry I am, for you. And your wife. But you know, in a sense she was lucky – lucky, I mean, in that sometimes death in these cases is virtually instantaneous. It happened to a friend of mine in a field outside Guildford. His wife drove him to the hospital, fifteen minutes away at the most. He was dead before they got there. But you, with just your bicycles in Guadeloupe, managed to keep her alive! And back here. To Mr Rolls. He's worked a couple of miracles, has our Mr Rolls.

J. G. (*eagerly*) Yes, he said something about miracles – two miracles I think he said there'd been in the last few years – do you know anything about them?

Pat Yes I do. One of them was three years ago, when I'd just started, chap called Humphrey, I can't remember whether that was his first or last name – Humphrey something, something Humphrey. Very tall. White-haired. He cycled over a cliff in Cornwall. Not on purpose, I don't mean. He was caught in a fog. Trying to get out of it. Head down over the handlebars, legs pumping, vision impaired. So over he went, pedalling. On to the rocks below. Whole body smashed, including his head. He lay here – this very room, actually – for four or five months. I used to think it very sad that nobody but me ever visited him – except for his landlady, his landlady came once but only to try to get her rent. He seems to have been rather unpopular, at least according to her. He was a psychiatric nurse. Still is, I suppose. (*Stops.*)

J. G. Well, what happened?

Pat Sorry. Well, one day I popped my head around the door and saw that he was scowling. That was the first sign. Then he began to clench and unclench and clench his fists. Like a boxer. Guttural sounds from his throat. Barks, really. And then he was on his way. Extraordinary progress. Complete recovery. Apart from the occasional memory loss. That was Humphrey. The Humphrey miracle.

J. G. I see. And the other one? The other miracle?

Pat Sandy. A bonnie lass of nineteen. Went scuba diving. Got into a terrible tangle in a fishing net. Was assumed drowned when she was hauled out. Mr Rolls said that her brain was deprived of oxygen to the point where she should have been – no, he can't have said 'should', can he? – but normally she would have been past the point of no return. But her parents, her boyfriend, her friends, refused to give up on her. They kept at her and at her – they were Scots, so they did all kinds of Scottish things, reels and Highland flings, bagpipes, sang 'Auld Lang Syne', hogmanay, the lot. Pitiful, I thought it was, pitiful. Until one day, at tea-time, they were sitting around her eating freshly baked scones, laughing and joking as if they were picnicking somewhere in the heather, her eyes fluttered. She made a little cawing sound. She smiled. She was on her way back. Well, most of the way back. A good part of the way back.

3

J. G. Then Mr Rolls didn't really have anything to do with it? With either of them.

Pat Well, they were under his care. But I'm sure he wasn't claiming them as his miracles. Mr Rolls would be the first to attribute them to God. Or – or to a fluke. After all, that's the nature of miracles, isn't it, there's nothing to explain how they come about. Though that doesn't mean there isn't an explanation somewhere or other. Like the first car I had, an old Citroën – sometimes it would just stop itself for no reason any garage could discover – they'd change the battery, clean the plugs, fiddle with wires – and me, I'd kick at it, swear at it, beg it on my hands and knees – nothing. And then suddenly it would start up just like that, as if it felt in the mood again, almost. I used to think it was a miracle at the time – at least I always said 'thank God' – but it could have been a fluke. On the other hand there was probably a mechanical explanation, who knows? As Mr Rolls says.

J. G. Well – well, let's suppose there's an explanation for the two miracles you and Mr Rolls – what can I do? Tell me what to do.

Pat Well, what people usually do – and what might have done the trick for Sandy – is family. Family and friends.

J. G. Family and friends, yes. But – but the trouble is we haven't really got any. I mean – I mean, we've got friends of course, but they're lunch friends, dinner friends, that sort of friend. And there's Julia, my agent –

Pat Agent?

J. G. Yes, literary agent. She negotiates my contracts, that sort of thing. But she and Gwen weren't really particularly close. But the point is, there isn't really anyone –

Pat And no family?

4

J. G. No, none. Well, there's my brother, Jack. But he's – he's – well, we only see him occasionally. When he's in trouble. He's an actor, you see – and – and – the point is we're very private, Gwen and I. We cherish our privacy, you see.

Pat So it's just you then, is that what you're saying, Mr Golding?

J. G. Yes, that is what I'm saying. Just me when it comes down to it.

Pat Well, at least she's nicely settled down. And in a room all to herself.

J. G. Yes, but I don't think she can appreciate – I mean, she won't have noticed, will she? Or will she? (*With sudden hope.*)

Pat Well, as Mr Rolls always says – who can say? But at least you'll have your privacy together, won't you? That's the good thing.

J. G. Yes, yes, our privacy. But to do what? What do we do? What do *I* do, I mean?

Pat Well, I suppose you should do all the things you always do in your privacy. And hope that one day soon she'll come back from wherever she is all on her own to join in with you.

J. G. Yes, yes, right. (*Pause.*) I'll bring her back. I swear to God I'll bring her back!

Pat That's the spirit, Mr Golding. Because whether there are miracles or not, we still need faith.

J. G. I've got faith, I've got faith. (*Little pause.*) May I ask – what is your function? Your specific function?

Pat Oh, just to keep an eye on you is what it comes to.

J. G. On me?

Pat Yes. On your case.

J. G. On my wife's case, don't you mean?

Pat Of course on your wife's case. I'm really here to be around for when I'm needed.

J. G. Oh, I see. Well, thank you, thank you very much.

There is a pause. Pat, smiling pleasantly, J. G. wondering what to say.

Pat Well, if there's nothing else I'd better be off to the Wisdens. A lovely couple – well, I don't know about him of course, but from what she tells me, the way she dotes on him – even in his absence – he must have been quite a man.

J. G. Must have been? You mean – you mean –

Pat You're quite right, Mr Golding. Must *be*, must *be* – keep everything in the present tense here, eh? (*Exits.*)

Lights.

SCENE TWO

Lights down.

J. G. (*over*) It was hot, very hot. We'd been cycling for hours, and there we were on a country lane off the main road. She had to stop for a widdle. There was a buzzing. I was vaguely aware of the buzzing. It contributed to all the drowsiness, the heat, the peacefulness. But it must have alighted on her neck because suddenly there was no buzzing. She was about to get up when 'Ow,' she said. 'Ow.' And clapped her hand to her neck.

6

Lights up on Gwen, now seen properly. Six weeks later.

A small window, stage left, with a sofa under it. A bed upstage, with a chair on either side of it. Also a bedside table, with books, magazines on it. Downstage, a larger table with a couple of chairs. On this table sits a chessboard, more books, magazines, a compact disc–tape-recorder–radio. Stage right, a sink, a mirror, a razor, shaving foam, etc. In the corner of the room, on a shelf on the wall, a television set.

It is about ten in the morning. Spring day.

The television set is on, giving a summary of the news. The sound is low.

J. G. enters. He is wearing casual clothes, under a raincoat. He is carrying a bunch of white carnations, a newspaper. There is also a book in his pocket.

J. G. (*takes off raincoat, extracts book, puts it on the table, looking at the television set in disgust*) Oh, for Christ's sake – we would agree that you're not the liveliest company at the moment, but surely they can roll you about your bed, change your sheets, mop you up, unplug and replug your tubes, change your drip, drip, drip without needing to keep one eye on the television – (*Goes across to turn it off. His attention is caught by something on the screen. Picks up manual control, raises volume. He is still holding carnations, by the way.*)

TV – the number of dead has now risen to a hundred and twenty thousand. In Calcutta alone a quarter of a million people are thought to be infected. The British Government has closed the airports to all Far Eastern flights, both inward and outward bound. (*Little pause.*) At home, a London newsagent, Mr Lionel Patel, and his seventeen-year-old son, Sam, were shot dead by two men in balaclavas inside their shop in Shepherd's Bush. The victim's wife, Mrs Violet Patel, says –

7

J. G. (*turns off television*) See what we're missing, Gwen? Real life. And real death. How pleasant to be cocooned here, in complete safety. (*As he speaks, he puts the fresh carnations on the table, throws the old carnations in the vase into a wastepaper basket, fills the vase with water from the sink, puts the fresh carnations in the vase, stands looking at them uncertainly.*) I'm losing my nerve. About these, I mean. I know there's something floral you particularly loathe because of that time Uncle Percy got you alone in the garden when you were thirteen – so the smell always gives you the willies – (*Sniffs.*) Is it these? What are they, anyway? You know I can't tell one flower from another, except buttercups – I must remember to ask one of the nurses, the tall one with legs, probably – Lydia, I think it is, isn't it? She looks as if she knows about flowers. And lots of other things too, I expect. Actually, she's very nice, isn't she? You like her, don't you? Caring – wouldn't that be our word for Lydia? Yours, anyway. Mine would be attractive, yours would be caring. Caring young Lydia. Pat was telling me the other day – oh, of course, you were here, weren't you? – that they have a very short shelf life in this ward. The nurses, I mean. Because of the strain of seeing – (*Stops.*) And the more caring and attractive they are – some of the others, though – Rosie, for instance – look as if they could tough it out for decades. Already have toughed it out for decades, in Rosie's case. We don't fancy decades more of Rosie – (*Stops, takes book out of his pocket, puts it on the bed.*) There! The new paperback edition at last. Arrived this morning, *Bananas in Borneo*, if you glance at the back, you'll find some relishable puffs, 'Jeff Golding's witty and vivid travel . . . highly enjoyable . . . more delightful for being offered . . .' that's the *Financial Times*. And here's the *Guardian*. 'The intrepid J. G. has pulled off another of his small miracles. His eyes and ears ever on the alert, his style effortlessly dead-pan, he carries us through the comedies and horrors of an alien land.' (*During this, goes to sink, begins to shave.*) 'But then J. G.' – notice that, darling, not Jeff Golding, or Mr Golding, or mere Golding, but J. G. – institutionalized by initials, that's what I'm turning into, a national institution – anyway, a kind of pet – what do you say to that? Comment, please. (*Glances towards bed.*) Comment, darling. Please. (*Goes back to shaving.*)

J. G. (*in Gwen's voice*) Fraud! Fraud! You're a fraud, Jeff!

J. G. (*shaves away*) Bit cryptic, that. Can you explain?

J. G. (*in Gwen's voice*) You could write the same book out of going up to Muswell Hill to do the Saturday shopping, you can't tie your shoe-laces without making a panto out of it, so when you're finished congratulating yourself on becoming an institutional buffoon, perhaps you'll come over here and give your non-suffering wife a little attention. I've had to get through another night without you. And without a drink. Which is worse.

J. G. You've been without a drink for over three years.

J. G. (*as Gwen*) That's what you think.

J. G. I don't want to know. There's no point in knowing.

J. G. (*as Gwen*) And now it's too late to find out. (*Laughs.*)

J. G. No, it isn't! It is not, Gwen. That I don't want to know doesn't mean it's too late to find out.

J. G. (*as Gwen*) Well, I've been without you for – for – how long has it been, Jeff? That I've been without you for?

J. G. You've never been without me. Not for a minute. It's you that's been absent. These last six weeks. For the

9

last six weeks I've been here. But you've been away. (*Pause.*) I believe – I'm determined to believe that it's been three years since you last drank. That afternoon at Simon's. That was the last time – and what a last time that was, eh? For both of us. For Simon too, come to that. Not that he noticed, I expect, he never notices, but still he did come down to see you – I mean, weren't you amazed? I was. Coming through the door, smiling vaguely, but actually getting your name right most of the time – not that he used it often as he scarcely spoke, but he looked benevolent, quite loving. And at least not at all embarrassed like the rest of them – Davina and Roger and Liza trying to avert their eyes from both of us, not knowing what to say to either of us. I hope I made it clear that there's no point, absolutely no point, in their coming back. Though Simon would be all right. I mean, after a time we'd scarcely know he was here, would we, and he was the only one who didn't ask – typical of him, I suppose – about what happened, so I didn't have to go through the bee saga all over again – (*Stops.*)

Pat enters unnoticed by J. G., who continues.

J. G. (*as Gwen*) Your fault! All your fault! (*Voice shaking.*)

J. G. (*finishes drying face, stares into mirror*) Yes. My fault. Yours too. *Our* fault. The way it should be between husband and wife. In sickness and in health. Sharing the fault. (*Turning around towards Gwen, sees Pat.*)

Pat (*cheerfully*) Morning, J. G.

J. G. (*startled*) Oh – morning, Pat.

Pat I didn't know you were in yet.

J. G. I popped into your office but you weren't there.

Pat Really? Oh yes, it must have been during the little

burst of excitement. Mr Wisden – his wife claimed she heard him singing the chorus from the 'Messiah'. He used to do it whenever he felt particularly chipper. Which was most of the time. She couldn't bear it, she told me, his voice baying out Hallelujahs all over the house. Now, of course, she'd give anything to hear them again. His Hallelujahs.

J. G. Well, and she has, you say.

Pat No, no, I'm afraid it was her own Hallelujahs she heard. I didn't know you shaved here.

J. G. I've just been trying it. These last few days. I thought it might – well, touch something. We did it every morning, you see. She would stay in bed while I shaved. We'd keep the door open and talk of – of this and that. Her day, my day. Monologues from one side or the other. Complaints. Jokes, quite often. Sometimes rows. So – so –

Pat (*going over to Gwen, stares down thoughtfully*) Oh, did I tell you – I'm having a great time with *A Chump in China*. Sometimes I laugh out loud. And what did Mr Rolls say today?

J. G. Nothing much. No change, anyway. Though he thought he noticed a smile. He was quite interested in that. Not excited. But quite interested.

Pat A smile. (*looking more closely at Gwen*) A smile. It looks more like a – (*thinks*) a smirk to me.

J. G. Yes, to me too. Odd, she never smirked in life. I mean, in ordinary life. But whether it's a smile or a smirk, perhaps it means she dreams. But Mr Rolls's view is that it's probably merely a slight muscular change, a nerve twitching. But I'm not so sure, I've caught one or two expressions – strange expressions – it's true I don't recognize them – well, anyway.

Pat You're doing a marvellous job, J. G. Nobody could do more, give more –

There is a knock on the door.

J. G. What? I thought we'd done them all. Come in!

Jack enters. He is holding a bouquet of flowers. He is dapperly dressed.

Oh, it's you. Of course. (*to Pat*) This is my brother, Jack. (*to Jack*) This is Pat. Dr O'Brien.

Jack and Pat nod to each other.

Jack I'm sorry I haven't looked in before but I – well, I wasn't sure – wasn't quite sure what the form is in – in these – (*Gestures towards Gwen, without looking at her.*)

Pat The form?

Jack Yes. (*to J. G.*) I've been waiting for a – well, to hear from you. An invitation. Or something.

J. G. Invitation! 'Dear Jack, I'd like to invite you to a party to celebrate our return from Guadeloupe. 6 p.m. Drinks and canapés. Dress informal. R.S.V. P. Intensive Care Unit, St Michael's Hospital, Paddington.'

Pat (*laughs*) Well, I'd better be on my way, I've got to look in on Martin's parents. The little boy in the car crash. They usually want to talk about insurance. But then everyone has their own way of dealing – I'll look in later on, for the usual. If you're up to it.

J. G. Yes, yes, of course. Looking forward to it.

Pat goes out. There is a pause.

Well, now you're here, do come and say hello. You haven't seen each other since – since – Gwen darling, here's Jack come to see you at last – my brother – remember him?

Jack holds out flowers to J. G.

For me?

Jack Well, for – for – (*Nods towards bed.*)

J. G. Then give them to her. (*Gestures to bed.*)

Jack hesitates, goes to Gwen's bed, looks down. Is clearly upset. Turns away. Puts flowers on the table.

Jack What's the prognosis?

J. G. Well, Jack, being a vegetable is a grey area. One day, who knows when, she may judder upwards into animal life. Alternatively, she might sink downwards into death. Or she might remain where she is now, for years. That's the prognosis.

Jack And all because of a wasp. A bloody wasp.

J. G. It was a bee actually. And now that we've covered our side of things, you can tell me why you've really come at last.

Jack What do you mean?

J. G. Here – let's sit down properly. (*Goes over to chair on one side of the bed, gestures to the chair opposite.*) We don't want Gwen to be left out.

Jack comes hesitantly over, sits down.

Off you go then.

Jack says nothing, his eyes fixed over Gwen.

The sound of your voice, you see. It might stir something. Are you resting?

Jack What?

J. G. I meant professionally. Are you resting again?

13

Jack Oh. Well, I suppose – I was in something at the Kennel. That pub theatre in Islington.

J. G. What was it about?

Jack An Aids play. It's become a genre, you know. But quite sharp and touching, I thought. So did most of the reviewers. I had a nice little part. Well, more than little. I survived into a bit of the second act. Two good speeches. (*Stops, unable to continue.*)

J. G. Pity we didn't get to see it, eh, darling?

Jack Oh, you wouldn't have enjoyed it much. Nor would Gwen. Neither of you like the plays I very occasionally get offered. Though I was quite good in it. Even if I did over-rehearse myself. As is my tendency, you once told me.

J. G. Actually, that wasn't me. That was Gwen. Wasn't it, darling? She always said that you acted as if you were directing yourself, so you should direct really talented actors who would listen to you but still be their spontaneous selves. Does that put it accurately, darling? (*to Gwen*) That he can't really act himself because he over-reacts to his direction of himself. The actor in him is awed by the director in him and –

Jack You're repeating yourself.

J. G. No, no, I'm repeating Gwen. But what we want to know is what happened to the Aids play, don't we, darling, it just closed, did it? No future?

Jack Oh, it's got a future all right. A West End management has taken it up. There'll be a short break and then it moves in.

J. G. But that's splendid, splendid, did you hear that, darling? Jack's bound for the West End again. At last. It's been – what? – ten years since you graced the boards, in the revival of that musical – Cockney Sparrow you were, weren't you? And now here you are, back again, dying of Aids and in the West End –

Jack I'm not going to grace the boards, dying of Aids in the West End. They've taken the short break to recast a few of the parts, mine among them.

J. G. (*looks for support to Gwen*) Oh. Oh, dear. What a – a pity.

Jack Gwen's quite right. I'm a rotten actor.

J. G. Anything in the offing?

Jack I've got an audition this afternoon.

J. G. What for?

Jack Cockney Sparrow's father. They're doing a revival. A touring revival. They hope to end up in London. But if they do, I won't be with them. They'll recast me. That's for sure.

J. G. Don't be sure, Jack. Nothing's for sure. That's what we've found out, haven't we, darling? Oh, and how's Esmond? You're still together? In your Hackney bedsitter?

Jack Yes.

J. G. Gwen thinks you're one of the cosiest couples she's ever heard of, eh, darling, from the way you describe yourselves. Sometimes we're actually quite jealous, aren't we? Oh, do tell us again about the way you met. You never know, it might, it might – (*nodding towards Gwen*).

Jack says nothing.

Jack Oh, for God's sake, Jeffie!

J. G. Well, I'll tell it. You met when he tried to mug you.

15

There he was, Esmond, a black tearaway from Notting Hill Gate, no future, no family, running with the pack, streaming along the pavements, snatching handbags from old ladies, mugging, drugging – you saved him from a life of crime, an early death – and think, it all began then, when he held a knife to your stomach. It takes most couples years to get to that point. But you saw something in each other's eyes, isn't that the way you tell it, doesn't he, darling? The sinner saw the saint, the saint saw a – what did you see, Jack? In Esmond's eyes, as he stood there in the darkness, your back to the wall, his knife to your stomach? More than the possibility of your death in the form of a beautiful young black –

Jack I saw a frightened boy.

J. G. So you took his knife away, and ushered him into your heart. And then back to your little flat in Hackney. Where you became the cosiest couple you've ever heard of, darling, from the way he tells it, eh, darling?

Jack Jeffie, what are you doing?

J. G. Counting your blessings. Which is one more than we have, isn't it, darling? But we aim to get ours back. Don't we, darling?

Jack (*after a pause*) It may interest you to know that my own blessing is currently in jail.

J. G. But you just said you were together.

Jack Of course we're together. In the sense that matters. He didn't *choose* jail instead of me.

J. G. What did he do?

Jack He went to the job centre, as he does every morning. On his way home. He was stopped by a couple of policemen. They started to manhandle him, incited him to

16

violence, that's what it really was – an incitement to violence – and for once he lost control – I'd told him, told him and told him to be passive, polite, deferential, just for a few disgusting minutes, and he'd managed it time and again but – I suppose he was depressed, no job on offer, no prospect of a job – and then being mauled and abused for absolutely no reason, apart from being black and young and jobless. They handcuffed him and took him to the station. And of course they found a knife on him, all kinds of dope, which of course wasn't his.

J. G. He'd stolen it?

Jack No, they planted it on him. And the knife.

J. G. You can be sure of that?

Jack I watched him dress before he left. (*Little pause.*) As a matter of fact I dressed him. One of our little rituals. So I know what he had in his pockets.

J. G. But he might have stopped off somewhere on the way to the job centre. Or on the way back. You can't even be positive he went to the job centre – sorry, darling, but it's got to be said. Whatever you think about men in uniforms. Women too – some of them are honest. Mean well. They do – try to do the decent thing, darling. As you know. From your own experience. (*as if jogging Gwen's memory*) With your drunk-driving charge? How long's he going to be in jail?

Jack I don't know.

J. G. Well, what's his sentence?

Jack He hasn't gone to trial yet. He's been remanded in custody. He could be in for a year before he even comes before a court. Innocent until proved guilty. So he'll rot innocently away in the filthiest conditions, on remand, being punished as if guilty even if he's found not guilty.

17

And there's nothing I can do. Unless I can find him a solicitor. A paid one. Legal Aid's no good – they try their best, but they've seen it all too often – and if you can't offer bail because there isn't the money –

J. G. Ah. (*Looks at Gwen, nods slightly. After a pause*) How much?

Jack (*shrugs*) Two or three thousand. (*Looks away from J. G. towards Gwen without intending to. Looks away from her.*)

J. G. That's quite a lot.

Jack I certainly haven't got it.

J. G. I have. Haven't I? I wonder how much, though. Gwen knows all about that side of things. Why don't – why don't you ask her? If she agrees, I'll write you a cheque for three thousand. On the spot.

Jack Ask Gwen?

J. G. That's it. Her decision. Not mine. Put it to her, why don't you? See what you can sort out between the two of you. I won't interfere in any way. (*Gets up, goes over to other table, sits down, picks up magazine, opens it.*)

> *Jack stares towards him, in disbelief.*
> *There is a pause.*
> *Jack looks at Gwen, makes to speak again, then looks towards J. G.*

Jack But if she can't speak –?

J. G. Oh, you'll hear something. I'm sure you will. If you get her to listen. And then listen hard yourself.

Jack But how will you know?

J. G. Well, I'll listen hard too. And if I don't hear her, I'll hear from you what she's said. Won't I? (*Goes on* *reading magazine.*)

> *Jack, after a pause, leans over and forces himself to whisper to Gwen, awkward and embarrassed.*

Jack Gwen, Gwen, if you can hear me –

J. G. Don't be afraid of playing – or even preying – on her emotions. She's always a soft touch. Especially where you're concerned.

> *Jack hesitates. Tries again. Begins to gesture.*
>   *J. G. watches him surreptitiously, over the top of the magazine.*

Jack (*becomes increasingly eloquent, gesticulatory, then stops, stares down at Gwen, smiles gratefully, bends over her*) Bless you, Gwen. Bless you. (*Gets up, goes over to J. G.*) Well, that's all settled then.

J. G. The whole whack? The full three thousand?

Jack Yes. Well, actually, she wants it to be three and a half thousand. So there's a little in hand after I get Esmond out.

J. G. Well! Well, well, well!

Jack (*boldly*) Isn't that right, Gwen? Three and a half thousand?

J. G. (*goes over to Gwen's bed, bends over it*) Is it right, darling? Three and a half? (*Little pause.*) What? Oh, I see. I'll clarify that then. (*Comes back to Jack.*) A little misunderstanding. She meant half the three thousand, not three and a half thousand. We're sorry. Oh, but look, you don't think you overdid it? The presentation, I mean. The actor/director taking over – rather than Jack just being Jack. Have another go, why don't you?

> *Jack makes as if to refuse.*

Think of Esmond rotting away.

Jack (*goes back, sits down on the bed*) Gwen, I haven't got anything to say, really. I've said it all. I can't bear life without him. That's what it comes to. And I'm so frightened for him in there. I'm desperate, Gwen. That's all it is. Will you help me? Please. Help us. (*Waits, then comes back to J. G.*)

J. G. And?

Jack Why don't you ask her? To avoid any further misunderstanding.

J. G. (*goes to the bed*) He *is* my brother, darling. And though we don't – of course we don't believe a word he says, and never have – about why he needs it, we are in the habit of letting him have it. You always say it's worth it, just to find out what story he'll come up with next. And Esmond in jail is quite a good one. Far better than his last – the need for an immediate operation on his vocal chords that he couldn't get on the National Health, so – so – (*as if listening*) oh, darling! What a sister-in-law I've acquired for my brother. (*Kisses her, strokes her head.*) Oh, I'm sure he will. (*Comes back to Jack, who has sat down. Sits down, takes out a cheque book, writes a cheque.*) What *do* you want it for?

Jack I told you – (*Stops.*) I need it to pay off my overdraft. To pay my back-rent. And to pay the landlord for the damage that little shit and his friends did to my flat when he left. Graffiti on the walls, smashed furniture, urine and crap on the carpet – there. Satisfied?

J. G. Yes, I am. I find that a much more moving story (*handing him the cheque*).

Jack (*takes cheque, puts it in his pocket*) Thank you.

> *J. G. nods towards Gwen.*

Jack nods thanks towards Gwen.

(*to J. G.*) I never thought you believed my stories, only
that you pretended to accept them to save me – save me –
well, I didn't tell you the truth this time either. The fact of
the matter is I want the money for a two-man show
Esmond and I are going to put on at the Edinburgh
Festival. That's the fact of the matter, Jeffie. But as it is –
I'll take my chances as Cockney Sparrow's father. I don't
want anything (*taking cheque out of his pocket, tearing it
up*) from you again. (*Carries the bits of cheque over to
bed.*) Either of you. (*Realizes.*) What am I doing? (*Goes to
door, turns as if to say something, goes out.*)

> *J. G. sits down at table. Hums, taps his foot, picks up
> magazine.*

J. G. (*after a little pause*) Did you say something, darling?
(*After another pause.*) Mmmm? (*After another pause.*)
Anyway, you don't have to. I know what you're thinking.
That I shouldn't have forced you to take the decisions.
That's it, isn't it, darling?

J. G. (*as Gwen*) It was disgusting. Quite disgusting.

J. G. Yes, but he can't help it. Couldn't help it. Perhaps
he can from now on.

J. G. (*as Gwen*) No, you were disgusting. You used me.

J. G. No. He tried to take advantage of you. And you let
him.

J. G. (*as Gwen*) You let him. I'd never have done that to
him. You enjoyed yourself.

J. G. Perhaps. But at least he tore up the cheque for once.
For once he did the manly thing –

J. G. (*as Gwen*) Manly!

J. G. Grown-up then, that's how you'd put it. Grown-up! Hah!

Gwen (*as herself*) I'll speak for myself, if you don't mind.

J. G. (*suppressing a grin of pleasure and triumph, seeming still to concentrate on his magazine*) Then go on, darling. (*Yawns slightly.*)

Gwen I hate it when you're unkind. You're not unkind. It's not in your nature to be unkind.

J. G. Oh, I think it must be. Between us we're bringing it out. Besides, if you didn't like it, you should have stopped me, shouldn't you? Just one word would have done the trick.

Gwen And what word would that have been?

J. G. How can I say? It would have been *your* word. You ask me to let you speak for yourself, and then you ask me to put words in your mouth.

Gwen No. You choose to put them there, as you're doing now. There are no words in my mouth, no hearing in my ears, no thoughts in my head, no impulses in my heart.

J. G. Then how come you're speaking to me? And how can you speak to me if you can't hear what I'm saying, can't think about what I've said, can't feel some impulses in your heart?

> *There is a silence.*
> *J. G. goes over, kisses Gwen on the forehead, takes her hand, sits down beside her, stares at her, kisses her again. Picks up newspaper.*

Ah. A seventeen-year-old's been picked for Sussex –

(*as Gwen*) Oh, please not the sports pages.

(*tosses newspaper aside*) OK, not the sports pages. So

where does that leave us? (*Goes to tape machine, picks up tape.*) Shall we do household noises again? If they weren't familiar to you when you were at home, they've certainly become familiar while you've been away. At least to me. (*laughing*) Oh, I know – we haven't had this for a bit – not exactly seasonal but it always brings back memories. At least to me. (*Puts on 'Silent Night'. Picks up book, looks at quotes on back as lights go down*)

SCENE THREE

Lights down.

J. G. (*over*) I passed out. When I came to, they'd gone. Just me and the guards. The odd thing was I still had my passport and wallet. I was sure I'd been defiled in some way. While I was unconscious. But when the British Consul saw me in one of the prison offices and I told him that I'd been raped, he said that it was extremely unlikely, 'extremely unlikely', as the four other men in the cell were members of Amnesty, there on a conference, who'd asked if they could spend a night in prison to experience conditions for themselves.

Lights up.
  Three weeks later.
  J. G. is sitting at table, looking at newspaper. A chessboard is set up nearby, in the middle of a game.

J. G. Hey – here he is again, that boy! He got six wickets against Hampshire. Six for thirty-one. All the guile of an old master – deceptive, looping flight, the ball cutting back, turning away, fresh-faced, grinning, cocky – well, they've got to be cocky, haven't they, that's the real deception – what?

23

J. G. (*speaking as Gwen, from the bed*) This isn't fair, you're just taking advantage. You know how I hate sports. Especially competitive sports.

J. G. Yes, yes, yes, I do know. (*still reading*) And I'm sick to death of hearing you say it. You don't mind being competitive when it comes to attracting attention to yourself, though, do you? Your behaviour at parties, for instance, in the days when you were an alcoholic.

J. G. (*as Gwen*) I'm still an alcoholic, don't forget. I'll always be an alcoholic. And so will you.

J. G. All right then, in the days when you were an alcohol-drinking alcoholic. You competed with every other woman in the room. Usually successfully. I mean, you were always the first to fall into one of my friends' arms or on to their laps.

Gwen (*as herself*) What about you? Working yourself into drunken rages, throwing your drink over girls' blouses so you could rip them off –

J. G. I did not rip them off. They took them off.

Gwen They wouldn't have if you hadn't soaked them.

J. G. For God's sake, it only happened once and it was decades ago! Why do you keep going back to it?

Gwen Because I only found out about it a few years ago.

J. G. Ah yes. And of course that's an incident you'd be wiser not to mention. That ghastly afternoon when you shamed me – and yourself – in front of Simon.

Gwen You were drunk too. Completely drunk when you came to get me at the police station.

J. G. I drank from despair. You drove me to it. And I wasn't the one charged with 'driving under the influence'.

You were bloody lucky not to go to jail.

Gwen Oh, Jeff, Jeffie, why are you dragging us through all that again? It was just a lapse. You said so yourself afterwards. We'd stopped drinking for years before then and we didn't drink again after then.

J. G. Didn't we? How do I know whether you drank or not? You say yourself that there's no way for me to know. And as I always let you look after the money – perhaps that's why you wanted to, eh? So I couldn't check on your booze bill.

Gwen You let me look after the money because it was the only thing I was good at. The only way I could – I could – share – (*voice trembling*) and we came through – oh, my darling, we've come through. Look at me, Jeff, look at me. We're talking about us and your eyes are fixed on the newspaper.

J. G. (*after a pause, not looking up*) He also got twenty-three not out. So an all-rounder in the making. An England prospect. Though born in Jamaica – what we'll end up with is two West Indian sides, one based in the West Indies, one based in England, playing each other, while some honky from Yorkshire or Middlesex brings on the drinks –

Gwen Why won't you look at me?

J. G. You know perfectly well why.

Gwen No, no, I don't. Why, why, why?

J. G. Because you'll stop talking. You won't be there again. (*Looks at her.*) See, Gwen. You've gone. When I don't see you I can make you up. Or you make yourself up. But when I attend on you – attend – (*Turns back to paper.*)

   There is a pause.

Gwen You can't imagine me.

25

J. G. That's right.

Gwen Does that mean you're in danger of forgetting me?

J. G. (*still reading*) No. That you're in danger of my forgetting you.

Gwen What would become of us then?

J. G. I could lead a life.

Gwen You haven't got a life to lead. Not without me.

J. G. Don't be too sure, darling. Oh, did I tell you, Julia's coming round today at three – four – some time today, I think it's today – she's got contracts and – well, you know Julia, always on the ball – (*glances quickly at Gwen, then back at newspaper*) here's the contrary story. Finglebury, forty-three-years-old Middlesex opening bat, scored his second century in three innings – (*There is a long pause. J. G. stares desperately down at the newspaper.*) Well, darling? Forty-three, his second century – (*Another long pause.*) Well, Gwen? Two centuries, three innings, forty-three-years-old.

  Another long pause.

Gwen Sorry, J. G. Can't think of anything to say. (*Little pause.*) Silly boy. Soppy darling.

J. G. We should have had children. Proper children. Just one would have done. As long as it'd been a sensible one. Even a foolish one would have been better than none.

Gwen I suppose you blame me for that.

J. G. No, I don't. I blame both of us. Or neither of us. Couldn't be helped.

Gwen According to you, nothing can be helped. Ever.

J. G. Nobody can work out the consequences of sex. Or

the lack of consequences. It's entirely random, how the sperm, the eggs sort themselves out – sometimes long-ago genes revive themselves in a fraction of a second, sometimes nothing at all revives itself – (*little pause*) in a fraction of a second.

Gwen Try looking at me. Hold me. Hold me in your eyes.

J. G. Your eyes are closed. Your mouth is sealed. You're nowhere, Gwen.

> *There is a knock on the door.*
> *J. G. looks at his watch, surprised.*
> *There is another knock.*
> *J. G. goes over to the door, opens it.*

You're early, aren't you? Or are you late?

Julia (*enters, carrying a brief-case*) No, I'm exactly on time. Aren't I?

J. G. Yes, yes, I expect you are, you always are. Hours tend to get a bit muddled up in here. Sometimes it seems like the same hour, the same long hour.

Julia How are you?

> *J. G. shrugs.*

No change then?

J. G. One lives in hope.

Julia (*awkwardly*) I've brought some contracts. (*Begins to open brief-case.*)

J. G. They're not why I asked you here.

Julia I know. But they've still got to be signed – there's the American mini-series and – and – do you really want to go through with this?

J. G. What have I got to lose?

27

Julia Well, perhaps – perhaps your marriage.

J. G. If there's still a marriage to lose I'm a lucky man, aren't I?

Julia Have you tried this with anyone else?

J. G. Who else is there to try it with – apart from Jack. I had a serious go with him without his knowing it, which means he was true to form, but nothing much came of it. Except that he missed out on a couple of thousand. I expect he'll be back for it. Well – (*Looks at her.*) would you do the honours, please?

> *Julia stares at him uncertainly.*

(*encouragingly*) Your move.

Julia (*after a pause*) Sorry, I can't. I feel sort of awkward. It seems – seems kind of indecent, really.

J. G. Oh God, I wish you wouldn't say 'sort of' and 'kind of'.

Julia Sorry.

J. G. No, I'm sorry. (*Looks at Julia.*) Please.

Julia Gwen, Jeff and I are lovers.

J. G. Look, I know it's difficult but I scarcely heard that myself.

Julia (*after a pause, loudly*) Gwen, Jeff and I are lovers.

J. G. (*loudly*) Have you got that, Gwen? Julia and I are lovers.

Julia Please forgive me, Gwen. I've always wanted you to know. Felt so guilty. Haven't we, darling?

J. G. Yes. Well, I have, anyway. Since – since the bee – I can't bear to think about it. It seems so treacherous now. So squalid and – and –

Julia Well, I hope it was never actually squalid. (*little laugh of anger*) And as for treacherous, I did everything I could to keep it between ourselves.

J. G. Yes, we really did our best to make it into a hole and corner affair.

Julia (*to Gwen*) I always knew that you were the one that came first.

J. G. That's true, darling. She meant nothing to me, darling, nothing at all. It was just when we were going through one of our rough patches, so of course I looked for something on the – and it seemed practical because she was my agent and a sort of friend. Sort of, kind of – (*to Julia*) this isn't quite panning out as I – planned.

Julia Well, you may not be telling Gwen anything but you're telling me a great deal. When we were in Tonga, for instance –

J. G. (*to Gwen*) We were only in Tonga the once, darling, I promise. I mean abroad together once. The rest of the time it was after lunch stuff in London, when we'd finished discussing contracts and deals –

Julia I used to cancel meetings – important meetings – so that you could have your 'after lunch stuff'. I mean, for Christ's sake, if we're going to confess to our affair, let's try and give it some – some dignity, or what's the point of the confession?

J. G. You're absolutely right. I apologize, darling. It did have a little dignity in as much as we were in love. For a time. Sexually and – we had fun together, didn't we?

Julia Well, I hope so. At least I tried to give you fun.

J. G. Well, I hope you got some fun too. At least your usual 10 per cent.

Julia makes as if to slap J. G., suddenly realizes.

(*studies Gwen's face*) Nothing. Nothing, nothing, nothing.
(*to Gwen*) Don't you mind that I was unfaithful? Don't
you – (*to Julia*) let's have another go. (*Thinks.*) Oh, yes,
I've got something. You know, all the time I was away in
all the places neither of you came to, I'd occasionally have
a fantasy. An erotic fantasy. That while I was cavorting
through Canada, meandering through Madeira, a clown
in Columbia, a sot in the Sudan, all on my ownsome,
making a mint for you (*to Gwen*) and 10 per cent for you
(*to Julia*) – the two of you were lolling in each other's
arms, whooping in girlish laughter, playing with each
other sexually, having rows in order to have reconcilia-
tions, loving and loving and loving – (*Looks at Julia
encouragingly.*)

Julia (*to Gwen*) Yes – yes, I imagined telling you about
him – about what we were up to. It would always be an
Italian restaurant. And you'd throw a glass a wine into
my face, heave your spaghetti into my lap – and after I'd
mopped myself up in the Ladies, we'd settle down, yes,
settle down, to enjoy our lunch. That's the truth of it. I
wanted to be your lover, not his. I wanted you in my
arms, not him, and – and – I can't, I can't go on with this.
I have a life, I have a past too. I'm not going to have them
falsified like this – emptied like this – even for – even for –
(*Turns away from bed, is crying slightly.*)

J. G. You know how much it meant to me at the time.
How much it still means to me. (*Goes over to Julia, wipes
her tears away.*) Oh, my darling, my poor darling, my
poor darling Gwen!

Julia (*laughs*) I hope you heard that, Gwen – oh, I do
hope you heard that. Because that really was the whole
story. Is the whole story. (*There is a pause.*) Oh, the contracts. (*Opens her briefcase, takes out contracts.*)

J. G. How's Maxi?

Julia He's dead.

J. G. Really? Oh, dear. How?

Julia He strolled under a bus.

J. G. Strolled? Strolled under it?

Julia Yes. It looked quite deliberate. But he'd been rather depressed. Fatalistic.

J. G. But do dogs commit suicide?

Julia Oh, yes. More often than you'd think. But it's not surprising, their best friend is man, don't forget. That's why they have an inner life. Maxi was introspective, gloomy by nature. Ate badly. Slept badly. Low self-esteem.

J. G. On the other hand, he may just have been jay-walking. Are you going to get another one? Dog?

Julia I'm keeping an eye open for a bitch. A good-natured, life-loving, dependent and dependable bitch. Whose best friend is woman.

They laugh intimately, then both look guiltily towards Gwen.
Julia hands J. G. contracts. J. G. takes them, then hands them back.

J. G. To hell with them. To hell with all contracts.

Julia nods, putting the contracts back into her brief-case, and goes out.
J. G. sits at main table, picks up magazine, glances at cover.

Ah, the television guide. In other words, our weekly guide to murder, pillage, rape. What a foul world. (*Gets up, goes towards window, looks out.*) So that was Julia and I as we were then and are now. Then what might we have been, you and I, if Julia and I – but what does it matter as you're not here to be anything. Even as you were. And I – and I – what a foul world. (*Stares out of window.*) There she is, going down the steps, back to the office, I suppose, her brief-case full of unsigned contracts – I should have signed them, it would've only taken a minute – and life goes on, doesn't it – and she does try to earn her 10 per – oh, there's Lydia! Caring and attractive. Well, let's face it at last, old cheese, not just attractive but sexy. Throbbingly sexy. And those legs! Sometimes I don't know where to look when she's changing you, in case you're looking at me looking at her legs. I can't say she seems particularly sexy at the moment. Not even caring. No, careworn is what she looks. Poor Lydia, poor, poor girl, day in, day out, death after death, that boy gone – (*Gwen lets out a long sigh.*) I wish you wouldn't do that. You used to do it at night, when you slept like a normal human being. Now it's a provocation. (*Gwen lets out a rasp. J. G. turns away from window.*) And you used to do that as well. I'd put my hand on your side, you'd let out a rasp of pleasure, of security and – I remember, through the fog of sleep, your hand – open your eyes, damn you. You have no right, no right –

> *He goes over to tape machine, puts on 'Silent Night', begins to hum with it, then, as Gwen, hums 'Silent Night'.*
>   *During this, Pat enters, stands, watching.*
>   *J. G., as Gwen, continues to sing 'Silent Night'. The effect is desperate and grotesque. J. G. stops, suddenly aware of Pat.*
>   *There is a pause.*

Just like your Mrs Wisden. Except Gwen's voice was rather lovely. At least it never bayed.

Pat May I? (*Going to sofa, sits down, begins to roll a joint.*)

J. G. It was her favourite carol. She used to sing it every Christmas. It was a tradition. She at the piano, I listening to her. And I keep remembering that Christmas –

Pat is vaguely studying the chessboard during this.

– seven – eight years ago? before I went to Tonga. For my first book. She looked so beloved, eyes wicked, her head back, not having to watch her fingers – oh, the sight of her, and yet I – it's the Hardy poem, isn't it, do you know Hardy?

Pat Yes, yes – 'kiss me, kiss me, Hardy' –

J. G. The poet. The poet. 'Everything glowed with a gleam; Yet we were looking away!' And that's it. I was looking away. Looking at her in joy, but within myself, looking away, looking forward to all the funny things I'd make sure happened to me as I trekked through Tonga – I even had the title before I went to bed, 'By Tube to Tonga', 'Silent Night' still in my ears –

Pat 'By Tube to Tonga'. (*Laughs, moves a chess piece.*)

J. G. – and then checking my knapsack, my plane tickets, my passport, my vaccination certificate, then – then to bed, where she lay reading, eyes half-closed, waiting, and still I could hear it, will never not hear her voice – even while I was looking away – just like Mrs Wisden – I wouldn't look away again. Not if she let me see her at the piano one more time. How long has he been gone now? (*Goes over to chessboard.*)

Pat Mmmm?

J. G. Mr Wisden. When was it he died finally?

Pat Three weeks, isn't it? Two, anyway.

J. G. So she's, um, liberated at last, is she? (*Sitting down at chessboard.*)

Pat N-no. Not really. Keeps coming back as if he's still alive. Completely baffled when she realizes. Spent all those months, you see, willing him, willing him, and now there's nothing left to will. But she still goes on willing. Like a muscle, you see. Keeps flexing itself.

J. G. (*moving a chess piece*) Sometimes I think you only come in here so you can dope yourself safely.

Pat That's only partly true. I also come in for this (*moving a chess piece*).

J. G. One of the nurses noticed the smell the other day.

Pat The tall, leggy one, very pretty. (*Nods.*) Very pretty. Linda.

J. G. Lydia. She smelt it and I could tell she knew what it was.

Pat Yes, I know. She reported you to me. I said that you were probably trying to reach Gwen through a favourite memory. I explained that people of your generation started the whole fashion. That's right, isn't it, you all did it, didn't you?

J. G. Just now and then, eh – (*Checks himself.*) We were a very old-fashioned couple. Stuck strictly to booze and tobacco. Until we gave them up.

Pat A dish, isn't she? Those legs –

J. G. I wouldn't know, I haven't noticed.

Pat Haven't noticed! Haven't noticed her legs! Her –!

   J. G. looks away, looks back at Pat, laughs. Pat laughs.

J. G. You respond to it very quickly, don't you?

Pat (*looks at his joint, inhales*) Yes, something in my chemistry, I suppose. The downside is that it wears off very quickly too.

J. G. So what are you going to say to Mrs Wisden?

Pat Nothing any more. I've sent her on to Mr Rolls, to explain the facts – well the fact. That her husband is dead. So it's his can of worms.

J. G. And how's he going to calm her down? Tell her that because she's missed out on one of his miracles, it doesn't mean that there isn't another one around the corner? A really big one. A resurrection! There isn't the bedside any more but there's always the graveside. Try baying out a few Hallelujahs there.

Pat (*studying chessboard*) Hallelujah. That's right. Keep the faith.

J. G. (*intensely, as if to himself*) Is there ever a time when one can say enough? Enough. I've had enough.

Pat Mmmm? (*Moves a chess piece.*) Check. No, mate, isn't it? Yes, it's mate. Hallelujah and amen.

Lights.

SCENE FOUR

Lights down.

J. G. (*over*) 'Quiete ya – silencio.' Then I was being dragged up the steps of some institution and hustled down a corridor, tossed into an ante-room, and left there with a couple of guards. I assumed – what was I to assume? – that I was going to be executed. I was crying, I think, yes, I'm afraid I was crying. And then he came in. The doctor. He was angry. I've never seen anyone so angry. He stood in front of me and another guard opened a door and some little man came in, unshaven, fat, cheerfully malignant he looked, and I thought – I thought – is this my executioner? But he was the interpreter, actually.

Lights up.
Jack is sitting beside Gwen, holding her hand to his forehead.
Pat is lying on sofa, apparently asleep.
J. G. enters, unshaven, carrying a carrier bag.

Jack I came to ask – to ask for – for your forgiveness. And Gwen's. I'm so ashamed, so ashamed. Ashamed at having failed you as a brother. A proper brother. I've been trying to imagine what it's like for you – well, of course I saw for myself. Crazed. Crazed with despair, that's what you've been, haven't you? (*Pause.*) Look, Jeffie, I'm going to talk. Brother to brother. About you. What's happening to you. What's going to become of you? I'm going to say what I've got to say whether you want me to or not. You can't go on in here, Jeffie, you can't. Look, I know how much you loved – love Gwen, and how much she loved – loves you. But she would have hated the thought of you in here every day. She would have wanted you to get on with your life. To get back to your work. Think of Daddy. How much he loved Mummy. When she was dying – all those months of ugly dying – and she was conscious for most of them, she could speak, could reach out for his hand – she insisted he got on with his life. She insisted on it. Into classes every day, marking papers every evening after he came back from the hospital. When the school offered him compassionate leave he refused to take it. She wouldn't let him. If we hadn't heard him sobbing at night, we wouldn't have known how deeply he felt – and then immediately after the funeral, back to the classroom. Getting on with his life saved his life. He told us so. And that's what Gwen would want for you. I mean, you're not blaming yourself, surely?

J. G., during this, has sat down and is writing a cheque.

Jack It was an accident. A one-in-a-million accident! You're not God, Jeffie, you can't – can't rule bees and know where they're going to visit and who they're going to sting and why they choose one person as opposed to another –

J. G. Over-rehearsed. Over-rehearsed, as usual. (*Hands Jack cheque.*)

Jack (*takes cheque, looks at it*) I – I –

J. G. She was widdling into the dust. By the side of the road. The bee alighted on her neck. She clapped her hand to her neck. 'Ow,' she said, 'Ow.' Bzzzzzz –! (*Slap.*) Ow! Bzzzzzz –! (*Slap.*) Ow! Bzzzzzz –! (*Slap.*) Ow! (*Begins to shake.*)

Pat (*to Jack*) I'll see to your brother. He'll be all right. I'll see to him.

Jack hesitates, pockets the cheque, leaves.
   Pat begins to roll a joint.
   J. G. winds down. Still trembling, he sees bottle in his hand, pours it down the sink, goes to chair, sits, huddled.

J. G. Sorry. Just my way of baying at the graveside.

Pat What? Oh, Mrs Wisden you mean. No, no, she's not at his graveside. Not at the moment anyway. She's in Majorca. I had a postcard from her this morning. Doing a lot of swimming, she says.

J. G. She was widdling into the dust. The bee alighted on her neck. She clapped her hand on her neck. 'Ow,' she said. 'Ow.' (*Pause.*) Over-rehearsed. A liar. Still, the truth will out, eh? (*Looks at Pat.*) It wasn't an accident, Pat.

Pat (*after a pause*) Ah. Is this a confession, then? Is that what I'm about to hear?

J. G. It was unbearably hot. We stopped at a café to have a lemonade, and instead of lemonade I ordered beer – the first time we'd drunk alcohol – well, together – for years. As far as I know. It went straight to our heads, as always, so – so there we were, the two of us, and the beer warm and flat, flies everywhere – on our eyelids, our nostrils – and there were some military types shouting and laughing – and when it came simmering up, why didn't I go and demand cold beer, and I said, what's the use, they won't have any, and she said, and I said, and so it went, until I don't know, we were snarling, snarling, on our feet snarling, and they'd gone silent, watching us – and suddenly one of them, the one with a scar, got up, pushed me out of the way, and told Gwen to shut up, stand still, 'Quiete, silencio,' that sort of thing, and she went at him, demented, and he took out his gun, and pointed it straight into her face – 'Ow!' she said. 'Ow!' And fell. And he – he unzipped his flies and stood over her, his cock in his hand, grinning down at her, grinning with the strain of trying to pee over her face – I grabbed a jug and smashed it over his head and – and – do you understand?

Pat (*who has surreptitiously lit another joint during this, nods seemingly dopily*) Yes, yes. Drew his gun to keep her still. Tried to urinate over her to neutralize the poison. And you buggered him up.

J. G. If it hadn't been for me, he might have saved her.

Pat But then how were you to know? Most people don't. Though everybody should. (*Nods to himself.*) Should. First aid handbook stuff.

J. G. But don't you see the joke? The joke of it?

Endearing old J. G. at it again. Heroically and comically preventing his wife's life from being saved. It's like one of the things I make up in my hotel rooms. Because that's how I really do it. I don't go out and about on bicycles looking for trouble, getting involved in scrapes and mis-understandings, getting myself lost – I hate trouble of any kind, I always have. Except the trouble I make up in my hotel rooms. I just sit there, in an armchair if I'm inside, or in a deck-chair on the terrace, speaking into my tape recorder, making up trouble. So she's quite right to call me a fraud. That's what she calls me, you know – some-times as a term of endearment, her 'little fraud', some-times – sometimes to wound me. So when she insisted on coming with me for once, it just seemed like vindictive-ness. Typical, I thought. So I responded vindictively. For the first time I really did do all the things I'd only pre-tended I'd done – I hated every minute of it – and so did she – cycling in the heat, actually getting lost, rows in the bank over the rate of exchange – but even so I would have made it all a good read. Highly entertaining. Even the bit about my wife being stung – she'd have been my partner in buffoonery. That would have been my revenge. And she'd have laughed, I know she would. So it would have been a nice revenge, the two of us laughing at ourselves. Back home. (*Pause.*) My last words to her were full of poison.

Pat But that doesn't matter. You love each other. That's what matters.

J. G. We don't love each other enough to love her back to life. So what is the good, what is the good of our love if it's got poison in it and no antidote?

Pat Well, that's it really, isn't it? That's the whole issue, the fundamental question itself. I mean, look at you, J. G., going on and on, on and on creating, recreating her out of the void in this room, the void on the bed, the void in yourself – and all the time you're asking the fundamental question. Why do we have to love if love is the cause of our greatest suffering? Without love there'd be no grief, no guilt, and above all, no hope. That would be the best of it – no hope. Then you'd be free, wouldn't you? Free to move on. Goodbye Gwen, hello Lydia.

J. G. (*stares at him in momentary disbelief*) Goodbye Gwen, hello Lydia!

Pat Well, it's goodbye Lydia too, as a matter of fact. She asked to be transferred to another ward. Much better hours too. So I might make a move soon. Been on my mind. Though I've heard she's tangled up with some married bloke.

J. G. Tell me – is this what you do with the others? What you did with Mrs Wisden and the parents of that boy? Sit smoking a joint, rambling on about the hopelessness of their love, planning your – your sex life? Do you play chess with them too? Is that really all you have to offer any of us?

Pat Well, yes, J. G., that's what I have to offer. Though you're the only one I play chess with. I used to play Scrabble with the Norris twins – well, they were triplets actually, but the third one was in bed – and Beggar My Neighbour with –

J. G. And that's the point of you, is it, the whole point of you? That's what you're employed to do?

Pat Oh, no, J. G. The point of me is you. You're the point of me. You see?

J. G. No, I don't see.

Pat I'm doing research on people in your sort of condition. How you all cope and fail to cope. Well, we might learn from it. The more data we get the more likelihood there is that we'll eventually be able to help people in your sort of condition.

J. G. And are you going to get a book out of it?

Pat I've published a few articles and one day, who knows, as Mr Rolls says. But don't worry, I shan't be using any names – just case numbers or alphabetically – Case one or two, Case A, Case B –

J. G. Are you saying – are you saying that you've kept her alive just so that you could study me in my – in my –

Pat Oh, no, J. G. No, no. It's Mr Rolls that's keeping her alive. Or allowing her to continue. That's his work. Mine is to observe the consequences.

J. G. Observe, observe – how can you observe anything in your sort of condition?

Pat Well, that might be true. It's sometimes a strain, you know. It's more than I can bear sometimes. I need to relax myself. (*Sucks on his joint.*)

> *J. G. stares at him, goes over, snatches joint from Pat's fingers, sniffs it, then inhales.*

J. G. This isn't – what is it?

Pat It's very bad for my throat is what it is. Dry it makes it. Dry, raw and thirsty.

J. G. It wasn't yourself you were trying to relax, it was me. Is that it?

Pat I was trying to be – family, you see. So that you had someone to relax with. It's not just for my career, J. G., it's for you too.

J. G. Family. My family's there. On the bed.

Pat Now is the time you can say enough. You've had enough.

J. G. Yes, I've had enough. Enough of you. So go, please. Please go.

Pat gets up, goes to door, turns.

Pat Look, you're not serving a custodial sentence. You're free at least to give yourself a break. Take a holiday.

J. G. But if I did and she did one or the other, I wouldn't be there to be with her, would I? But you would. And I wouldn't like that. (*Turns, begins to put away chess set.*)

Pat goes out.
J. G. puts away a few more pieces, then suddenly goes over to Gwen, kneels beside her, presses her hand to his forehead.

Oh, Gwen, my darling Gwen, please – please – !

He gets up in desolation, goes back to chess set, puts a few more pieces away.
Gwen sings 'Silent Night, Holy Night'.
J. G. makes as if to turn towards her, remembers, forces himself to stand, not looking at her, as Gwen continues to sing.
On this, lights fade down.

SCENE FIVE

Lights down.

J. G. (*over*) 'Our little country can't afford to keep your vegetable.' He spat it out, full of anger and – and contempt, and there was the meaning coming at me, almost idly, from the interpreter. And they went to the door, the doctor and his interpreter, then stopped suddenly. He spoke again, his eyes fixed on me. Not angry eyes, now, but insinuating – a – a tempter's eyes.

Lights up on J. G. speaking into a tape recorder. On the table, a typescript, exercise book, pen, a bottle of whisky. He is holding a glass from which he is sipping as he speaks.

The door is open. Pat is at the door, watching and listening. J. G., who has his back to Pat, is not aware of him.

(*into tape recorder*) 'He says that probably in your country there are all kinds of laws that complicate situations,' the interpreter interpreted. 'If you wish – he can offer you the advantages of a primitive society.' Very off-hand, the interpreter was, but there were the other pair of eyes, the doctor's eyes. 'If you go now,' the interpreter interpreted, 'he will finish it for you.' Not a cruel man, the doctor, even when offering a cruel choice. I wonder if he knew it was cruel, how I'd go back to it – time and again. That decisive offer that I decisively – (*Becomes suddenly aware of Pat, turns off tape recorder. There is a pause.*) How long have you been there?

Pat I don't know. I was listening so I didn't mark the time. Am I allowed to come in?

J. G. You seem to be already in.

Pat Then may I sit down?

J. G. (*hesitates, then gestures towards sofa*) But no herbal cigarettes.

Pat Oh. Pity. I discovered I'd become quite addicted.

J. G. Well then, (*raising his glass to his lips in acknowledgement*) I suppose you'd better have one.

Pat Thank you. (*Rolls a cigarette.*) Though it isn't actually a herbal. It's the real thing.

43

J. G. And how's everyone else since we last spoke?

Pat Some have come, some have gone. So it's as usual.

J. G. And Mrs – Mrs –?

Pat Wisden. She stayed on in Majorca. Something's happened but I don't know what it is. Her last postcard was evasive – excited but evasive. A waiter, do you think?

J. G. And Lydia?

Pat Not much fun. No sex. By inclination she's a patient, not a girlfriend. Falls in love with people in your sort of condition.

J. G. Really? Lucky I didn't know, I suppose. So what do you do when you're together?

Pat She sits in fairly expensive restaurants grieving by proxy. I nod away uselessly.

J. G. And the married man?

Pat Not married, widowed. Got two grown-up children. Rethinking his whole life in Bermuda.

J. G. So you have a widow in Majorca and a widower in Bermuda and – what are you doing here?

Pat Rolls sent me.

J. G. But he looked in this morning. He didn't say anything in particular.

Pat No, there was nothing in particular to say. That's the point.

J. G. Wants to pull the plug, does he?

Pat nods.

And you?

Pat He's the miracle worker and he's lost faith. He's not a cruel man either, even though he's offering you a cruel choice too. Take it, J. G.

J. G. I'm used to it here. I'm getting on with my life and staying in touch with my past. What more could a man want?

Pat The past is memories. Let them live in you. And not as a lump on the bed. You don't have to hang around here for your grief, it'll come at you when it will – in Majorca, Bermuda, wherever you are. Anyway, where and when you least want it. That's the thing about grief, it –

J. G. What do you say to a game?

Pat (*after a little pause*) Well, it seems I've got nothing better to do.

> They move to the table, J. G. taking the bottle of whisky and glass with him, Pat sucking on his joint. J. G. puts a cassette into the tape recorder.
> They begin to set up the chess pieces. Pat picks up a black and a white piece, puts them behind his back, then holds them out in his fists. J. G. points to one of the fists.
> Curtain.